THE
COMPLETE
PRIVATE PILOT
WORKBOOK

asa INC.

6001 SIXTH AVENUE SO.
SEATTLE, WA 98108-3307

(206) 763-0277

ISBN 0-940732-42-4

TABLE OF CONTENTS

CHAPTER TWO
AERODYNAMICS

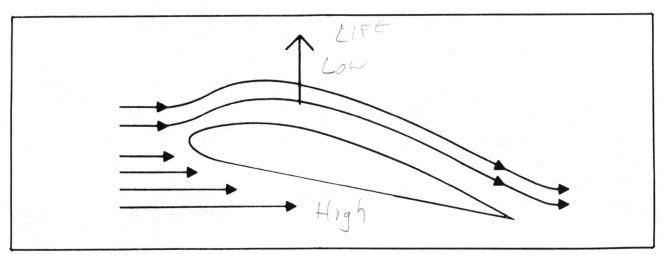

Figure W2-1.

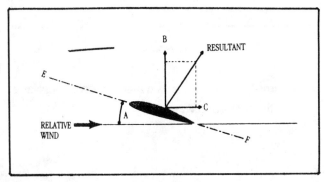

Figure W2-2.

1. On this airfoil (figure W2-1), identify the area of high pressure, the area of low pressure, and the force represented by the arrow.

2. Refer to figure W2-2.
   Angle A is the _Angle of Attack_.
   Arrow B represents _lift_.
   Arrow C represents _drag_.
   Line E-F is the _chord line_.

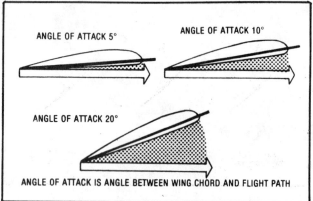

Figure W2-3.

3. Of the three angles of attack illustrated (figure W2-3), which would develop the most lift?

   10 ° angle of attack

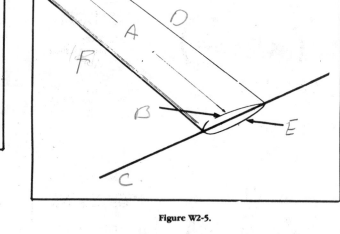

Figure W2-5.

E.   Lower camber
F.   Leading edge

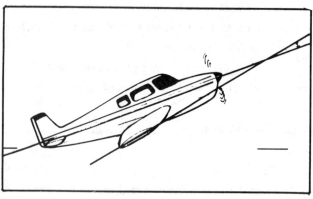

Figure W2-4.

4. What is the name of the angle illustrated (figure W2-4)?

   Angle of incidence

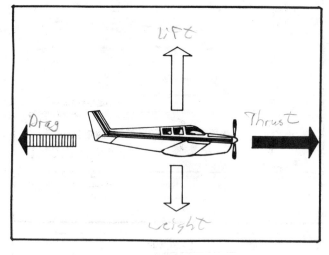

Figure W2-6.

5. Refer to figure W2-5. Connect each letter with the appropriate name.

   A.   Wing Span
   B.   Upper camber
   C.   Chord line
   D.   Trailing edge

6. Identify the four forces which act on an airplane in flight (figure W2-6).

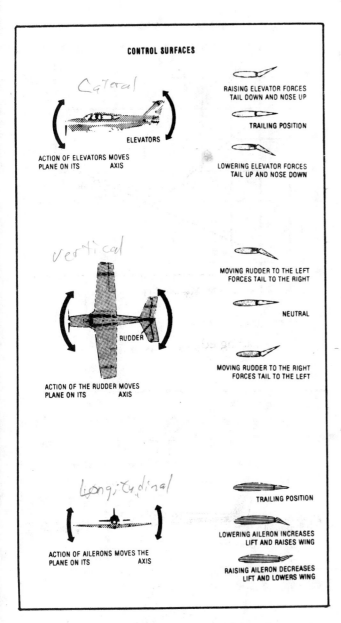

CONTROL SURFACES

Lateral

RAISING ELEVATOR FORCES
TAIL DOWN AND NOSE UP

TRAILING POSITION

ELEVATORS

ACTION OF ELEVATORS MOVES
PLANE ON ITS   AXIS

LOWERING ELEVATOR FORCES
TAIL UP AND NOSE DOWN

vertical

MOVING RUDDER TO THE LEFT
FORCES TAIL TO THE RIGHT

NEUTRAL

RUDDER

MOVING RUDDER TO THE RIGHT
FORCES TAIL TO THE LEFT

ACTION OF THE RUDDER MOVES
PLANE ON ITS   AXIS

Longitudinal

TRAILING POSITION

LOWERING AILERON INCREASES
LIFT AND RAISES WING

ACTION OF AILERONS MOVES THE
PLANE ON ITS   AXIS

RAISING AILERON DECREASES
LIFT AND LOWERS WING

Figure W2-7.

7. Can you identify the axis around which each control surface acts? (See figure W2-7)

8. Refer to the illustration (figure W2-8) and assume that all three airplanes are making coordinated turns. Which statement is true?

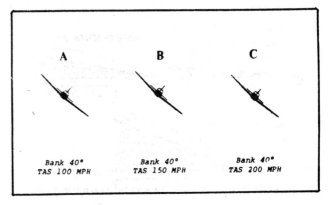

A   B   C

Bank 40°   Bank 40°   Bank 40°
TAS 100 MPH   TAS 150 MPH   TAS 200 MPH

Figure W2-8.

1. Airplane A will have the smallest rate of turn and the greatest radius of turn.

2. Airplane C will have the greatest rate of turn and the largest radius of turn.

3. Airplanes A, B, and C will have equal rates of turn, but airplane C will have the largest radius of turn.

4. Airplane A will have the greatest rate of turn and the smallest radius of turn.

ANSWER: _____

9. The force of ___drag___ acts parallel to the relative wind, while the force of ___lift___ acts perpendicular to the relative wind.

10. An airplane must ___stall___ before it will spin.

11. High relative humidity improves airplane performance because moist air is more dense than dry air. (TRUE / FALSE)

12. The center of pressure moves (FORWARD / BACKWARD) as the angle of attack is increased.

13. When an aileron is deflected into the airstream, the resultant _adverse___ _drag_ must be overcome by rudder pressure.

14. ___Parasite___ drag increases with airspeed, while ___induced___ drag decreases as speed is increased.

15. To counteract the effect of torque in a conventional single engine propeller-driven airplane, a pilot would normally add

    1. left rudder pressure during the takeoff roll and while climbing with full power.
    2. right rudder pressure when entering a glide from level cruising flight.
    3.) right rudder pressure during the takeoff roll and while climbing at full power.
    4. left rudder pressure when entering a climb from level cruising flight.

16. Select the true statement concerning the use of flaps during the approach for a landing.

    1. The use of flaps increases the airplane's stability.
    2. The use of flaps permits a decreased approach angle.
    3.) By using flaps, a steeper than normal angle of descent is possible without increasing the airspeed.
    4. The use of flaps requires a higher than normal indicated airspeed on the final approach.

LOAD FACTOR CHART

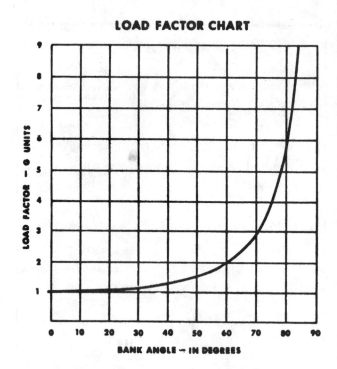

Figure W2-9.

17. Use the chart (figure W2-9). If an airplane weighs 2,300 lbs., what approximate weight would the airplane structure be required to support during a 60° banked turn while maintaining altitude?

    1. 3,400 lbs.
    2.) 4,600 lbs.
    3. 2,300 lbs.
    4. 5,200 lbs.

18. Induced drag (INCREASES / DECREASES) as the angle of attack is increased.

19. As you slow your airplane from 120 KTS to 90 KTS while maintaining a constant bank angle, the rate of turn will ___increase___ and the turn radius will ___decrease___.

20. Trim tabs normally move (IN THE SAME DIRECTION AS / OPPOSITE TO THE DIRECTION OF) the control surface.

21. An increase in airplane weight will (INCREASE / DECREASE) the stall speed.

22. The action of dihedral in raising an inadvertently lowered wing contributes to _Lateral_ stability.

23. Which statement is true regarding stalls?

    1. An airplane can be stalled only when the nose is high and the airspeed is low.

    2. An airplane can be stalled only when the airspeed decreases to the published stalling speed.

    3. An airplane can be stalled only when the nose is too high in relation to the horizon.

    4. An airplane can be stalled at any airspeed and in any flight attitude.

24. An airplane wing will stall only when the _Critical_ angle of attack is exceeded.

CHAPTER THREE
AIRCRAFT
ENGINES AND INSTRUMENTS

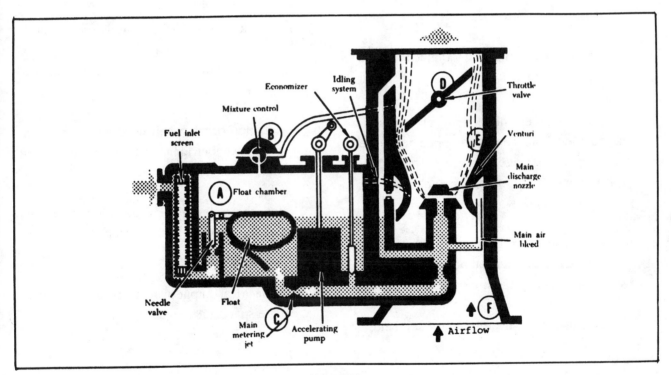

Figure W3-1.

1. Detonation can be caused by using fuel of a grade (HIGHER / LOWER) than that specified by the manufacturer.

2. Refer to the illustration (figure W3-1). Carburetor icing would be most likely to occur in which of the following areas?

1. Mixture control.
2. Accelerating pump.
3. Main air bleed.
4. Venturi.

3. If the engine oil temperature and cylinder head temperature gauges have exceeded the normal operating range, you may have been

   1. operating with the mixture set too rich.
   2. operating with higher-than-normal oil pressure.
   3. using fuel that has a higher-than-specified fuel rating.
   4. operating with too much power and with the mixture set too lean.

4. A fuel/air mixture containing too much fuel is a (LEAN / RICH) mixture.

5. Suppose that the engine oil temperature is normal, but the oil pressure has dropped below the normal operating range as indicated (figure W3-2). If the engine is running smoothly, the best procedure to follow would be to

   1. check the circuit breakers to determine if you have lost electrical power, and enrich the mixture to lessen the chances of detonation.
   2. continue to the nearest airport and land.

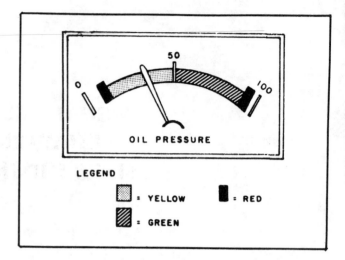

Figure W3-2.

   3. make a precautionary landing on the nearest stretch of straight highway.
   4. declare an emergency on the frequency 121.5 MHz.

6. Detonation occurs when hot spots in the combustion chamber ignite the fuel/air mixture in advance of normal ignition. (TRUE / FALSE)

7. When the unburned charge in the cylinders explodes, instead of burning normally, it is called _detonation_

8. The electrical output of an alternator varies with engine speed. (TRUE / FALSE)

CHAPTER FOUR
FLIGHT INSTRUMENTS

1. Which pitot-static instrument(s) would be affected if the pitot tube was clogged by a foreign substance?

    1. Altimeter and vertical speed indicator only.
    2. Airspeed indicator only.
    3. Airspeed indicator and altimeter only.
    4. Airspeed, altimeter, and vertical speed indicator.

2. Indicated airspeed corrected for position and installation error is _Calibrated_ airspeed.

3. True airspeed differs from indicated airspeed by _2%_ per 1,000' of altitude.

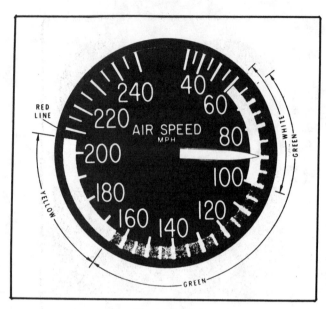

Figure W4-1.

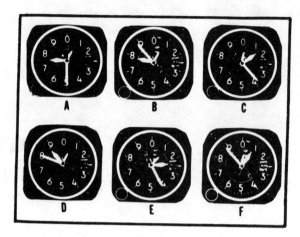

Figure W4-2.

4. Refer to the color-coded markings on the air-speed indicator (figure W4-1). What is the "caution range" of the airplane?

    1.   0 to 60 MPH.
    2.   100 to 165 MPH.
    3.   165 to 208 MPH.
    4.   60 to 100 MPH.

5. On a color-coded airspeed indicator the power-off stalling speed in the landing configuration is the (BOTTOM / TOP) of the (WHITE / GREEN) arc.

6. Refer to the airspeed indicator (figure W4-1). The maximum speed at which the airplane can be operated in smooth air is

    1.   100 MPH.
    2.   165 MPH.
    3.   65 MPH.
    4.   208 MPH.

7. Altimeter E (figure W4-2) indicates an altitude of

    12,400 _____ MSL.

8. Which altimeters (figure W4-2) indicate an altitude of more than 5,000 feet?

    A, B, D, E, _____

9. Which statement is true in regard to the effects of atmospheric conditions on the indication of a pressure altimeter? When flying in air that is

    1.   COLDER than standard temperature the aircraft will be higher than the altimeter indicates.
    2.   WARMER than standard temperature the aircraft will be at the altitude indicated on the altimeter.
    3.   COLDER than standard temperature the aircraft will be lower than the altimeter indicates.
    4.   WARMER than standard temperature the aircraft will be lower than the altimeter indicates.

10. When the altimeter setting is adjusted to 29.92 the altimeter indicates _pressure_ altitude.

11. Pressure altitude corrected for non-standard temperature is termed _Density_ altitude.

12. You depart an airport where the altimeter setting is 30.20" Hg, and fly to an airport where the altimeter setting is 29.94" Hg. If you have forgotten to reset your altimeter to 29.94 when approaching your destination, your altimeter will read _____ after landing.

    1. 26 feet high.
    2. 260 feet high.
    3. 26 feet low.
    4. 260 feet low.

13. The error in the indications of a magnetic compass caused by magnetic influences within the airplane is called (DEVIATION / VARIATION).

14. The actual speed of the airplane through the air is called _True_ airspeed.

15. Entering a right turn from a heading of 350°, the magnetic compass will initially indicate a turn to the (EAST / WEST).

16. When on final approach to runway 9, extending the landing gear and flaps will cause the magnetic compass to indicate a turn to the (NORTH / SOUTH).

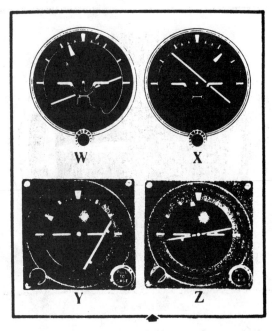

Figure W4-3.

17. Which attitude indicator(s) show the airplane in a right turn?

    _W, Y, Z_

18. Which instrument indicates a 40° banked turn to the left?

    _X_

19. Which instrument indicates a maneuver which is, by definition, an aerobatic maneuver?

    _Y_

20. In a slipping right turn, the ball instrument will be deflected to the (RIGHT / LEFT).

CHAPTER FIVE
WEIGHT AND BALANCE

1. When computing weight and balance, the "empty weight" includes the weight of the airframe, engine(s), and all items of operating equipment permanently installed. Empty weight also includes

    1. All usable fuel and oil, but does not include any radio equipment or instruments that were installed by someone other than the manufacturer.
    2. All usable fuel, maximum oil, hydraulic fluid, but does not include the weight of pilot, passengers, or baggage.
    3. the unusable fuel, hydraulic fluid, and un-drainable oil (or, in some aircraft all of the oil).
    4. all usable fuel and oil.

2. If baggage is moved from the aft baggage compartment (behind the passenger cabin) into the cabin, the center of gravity will move (AFT / FORWARD).

3. The distance from a weight to a reference point (or datum) is called its _ARM_____.

```
        PILOT'S OPERATING MANUAL
               (Excerpt)

AIRCRAFT DESIGNATION:-      BIRDCRAFT M-180
   (Four-place, Single-engine, Land Monoplane)

ENGINE OPERATING LIMITS:-   180 HP

FUEL SYSTEM:-         Float-Type Carburetor
                     91/96 minimum grade fuel
                     Fuel Capacity 30 gallons
                     in each wing tank (2 tanks)
                     58.8 gallons usable

OIL CAPACITY:-       8 quarts (not included in
                              empty weight)
PROPELLER:-          Fixed Pitch
LANDING GEAR:-       Fixed Tricycle Gear
WING FLAPS:-         0° to 35° Manual

EMPTY WEIGHT:-       1,446 lbs.
MAX. GROSS WEIGHT:-  2,450 lbs.

MAX. WEIGHT IN BAGGAGE COMPARTMENT - 120 lbs.
```

Figure W5-1.

4. Refer to the Pilot's Operating Handbook excerpt (figure W5-1). What is the combined maximum weight of four persons and baggage that can be loaded without exceeding the maximum certificated gross weight, if the airplane is serviced to capacity with fuel and oil?

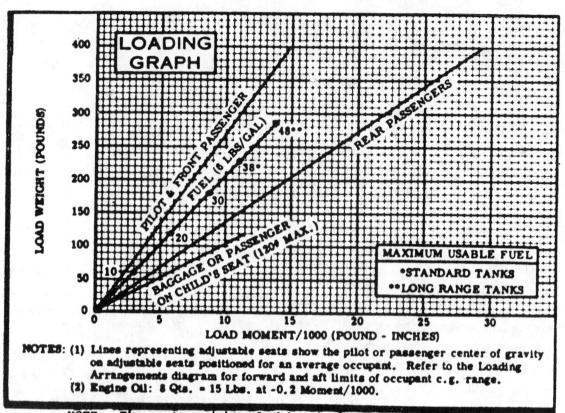

NOTES: (1) Lines representing adjustable seats show the pilot or passenger center of gravity
on adjustable seats positioned for an average occupant. Refer to the Loading
Arrangements diagram for forward and aft limits of occupant c.g. range.
(2) Engine Oil: 8 Qts. = 15 Lbs. at -0.2 Moment/1000.

NOTE: The empty weight of this airplane does not include
the weight of the oil.

DO NOT MARK ON CHARTS   USE PLASTIC OVERLAY

Figure W5-2.

1. 591 lbs.
2. 636 lbs.
3. 654 lbs.
4. 740 lbs.

5. Refer to the Pilot's Operating Handbook excerpt (figure W5-1). Assume you plan to load your airplane with 90 lbs. of baggage, 8 quarts of oil, and four persons whose total weight is 735 pounds. What is the total amount of usable fuel that can be aboard without exceeding the maximum certificated gross weight?

1. 16.5 gallons.
2. 27.3 gallons.
3. 29.0 gallons.
4. 31.5 gallons.

Use the Loading Graph and the Center of Gravity Moment Envelope (figure W5-2) to answer questions 6 through 8.

6.

GIVEN:	WEIGHT (LBS)	MOMENT/1,000 LB. INCHES
Empty weight	1,364	51.7
Pilot and front seat passenger	260	?
Fuel (30 gals. usable)	180	?
Oil (8 qts.)	15	-0.2

Based on the above information, what would be the center of gravity moment/1,000?

1. 69.9 lb. inches — utility category.
2. 75.0 lb. inches — normal category.
3. 51.9 lb. inches — utility category.
4. 55.1 lb. inches — normal category.

7.

GIVEN:	WEIGHT (LBS)	MOMENT/1,000 LB. INCHES
Empty weight	1,364	51.7
Pilot and front seat passenger	380	?
Rear passengers	250	?
Fuel (38 gals. usable)	228	?
Oil (8 qts.)	15	-0.2

With a maximum certificated gross weight of 2,300 pounds, based on the above, the aircraft is

1. within gross weight limit and within CG limits.
2. within gross weight limit, but exceeds forward CG limit.
3. over gross weight limit but within CG limits.
4. within gross weight limit but exceeds aft CG limit.

8.

GIVEN:	WEIGHT (LBS)	MOMENT/1,000 LB. INCHES
Empty weight	1,364	51.7
Pilot and front seat passenger	355	?
Baggage	90	?
Fuel (38 gals. usable)	228	11.0
Oil (8 qts.)	15	-0.2

What would be the gross weight and center of gravity moment/1,000?

1. 2,037 lbs.; 82.1 lb.-inches.
2. 1,940 lbs.; 80.1 lb.-inches.
3. 2,052 lbs.; 84.4 lb.-inches.
4. 2,200 lbs.; 85.3 lb. inches.

```
┌─────────────────────────────────────────────┐
│          PILOT'S OPERATING HANDBOOK           │
│                  (Excerpt)                    │
│                                               │
│  AIRCRAFT DESIGNATION:-        Raycraft 15    │
│   Single-Engine, Land Monoplane               │
│   (Seating Arrangement--Pilot and passenger   │
│   side-by-side plus a child's seat in the     │
│   baggage area)                               │
│                                               │
│  ENGINE OPERATING LIMITS:-     100 HP         │
│                                               │
│  FUEL SYSTEM:-     Float-Type Carburetor      │
│                    ●Fuel Capacity Standard Tanks - │
│                     two 13 gal. tanks         │
│                       (capacity 26 gals.) -   │
│                     maximum usable 22.5 gals. │
│                                               │
│                    ●Optional long range tanks -│
│                     total capacity 38 gals. - │
│                     maximum usable 35 gals.   │
│                                               │
│  OIL CAPACITY:-    6 quarts - included in empty │
│                    weight                     │
│                                               │
│  PROPELLER:-       Fixed Pitch                │
│  LANDING GEAR:-    Fixed Tricycle Gear        │
│  WING FLAPS:-      Electrically operated      │
│                      0° to 40°                │
│                                               │
│  EMPTY WEIGHT:-    1,104 lbs.                 │
│  MAX. GROSS WEIGHT:- 1,600 lbs.              │
│                                               │
│  MAX. WEIGHT IN BAGGAGE COMPARTMENT - 120 lbs.│
└─────────────────────────────────────────────┘
```

Figure W5-3.

Refer to the Raycraft 15 Pilot's Operating Handbook excerpt (figure W5-3) for questions 9 and 10.

9. What is the combined maximum weight of two persons and baggage that can be loaded, without exceeding the maximum certificated gross weight, if the airplane is serviced with 6 qts. of oil and the standard fuel tanks are full?

    1.   350 lbs.
    2.   355 lbs.
    3.   340 lbs.
    4.   361 lbs.

10. Assume the airplane is loaded as follows:

    Pilot . . . . 170 lbs.

    Passenger . . . . 125 lbs.

    Baggage. . . . . 65 lbs.

    Oil . . . . Full

    Fuel (standard tanks) . . . . Full

    This airplane is loaded

    1.   10 pounds more than the maximum allowable gross weight.

    2.   74 pounds more than the maximum allowable gross weight.

    3.   1 pound less than the maximum allowable gross weight.

    4.   10 pounds less than the maximum allowable gross weight.

For questions 11 and 12, the table method of center of gravity/moment solution will be used. The airplane has rear seats which can be either forward- or aft-facing, with a different arm for each. The data provided show how a solution is achieved for the following loading:

    Front passenger . . . . 150 lbs.

    Rear passenger (aft position) . . . . 135 lbs.

    Rear passenger (aft position) . . . . 160 lbs.

    Fuel . . . . 65 gals.

    Oil. . . . . 12 qts.

    Baggage . . . . 50 lbs.

The total weight is 3,183 lbs. and the total moment is 2,696 lbs., and these values are plotted on the envelope to show that the airplane is properly loaded.

FUEL

LEADING EDGE TANKS ARM 75

Gallons	Weight	Moment	Gallons	Weight	Moment
5	30	23	45	270	203
10	60	45	49	294	221
15	90	68	55	330	248
20	120	90	60	360	270
25	150	113	65 →390 →293		
30	180	135	70	420	315
35	210	158	75	450	338
40	240	180	80	480	360

BAGGAGE

ARM 150

Weight	Moment	Weight	Moment	Weight	Moment
10	15	100	150	190	285
20	30	110	165	200	300
30	45	120	180	210	315
40	60	130	195	220	330
50	75	140	210	230	345
60	90	150	225	240	360
70	105	160	240	250	375
80	120	170	255	260	390
90	135	180	270	270	405

OCCUPANTS

| FRONT SEATS | | | REAR SEATS | |
| ARM 85 | | | Forward Position ARM 121 | Aft Position ARM 136 |
Weight	Moment	Weight	Moment	Moment
120	102	120	145	163
130	111	130	157	177
140	119	140	169	190
150	128	150	182	204
160	136	160	194	218
170	145	170	206	231
180	153	180	218	245
190	162	190	230	258
200	170	200	242	273

EMPTY WEIGHT DATA

OIL NOT INCLUDED	Empty Weight (Lbs.)	Empty Weight Moment (/100)
Certificated Weight	2110	1652

OIL

ARM 25

Quarts	Weight	Moment
12	23	6

GROSS WEIGHT MOMENT LIMITS

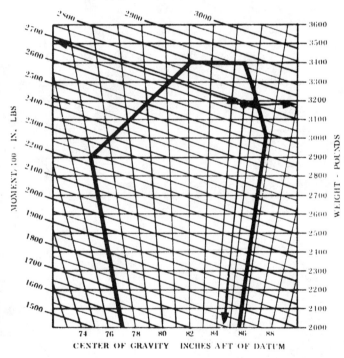

NOTE: All moments are equal to

$$\frac{\text{weight X arm}}{100}$$

Figure W5-3.

11. Using the table method, determine whether this loading falls within the operating envelope:

Pilot . . . . 180 lbs.
Front passenger. . . . . 155 lbs.
Rear passsenger (forward position). . . . . 130 lbs.
Rear passenger (aft position). . . . . 175 lbs.
Fuel. . . . . 75 gals.
Oil . . . . 12 qts.
Baggage. . . . . 175 lbs.

12. Determine if this loading is proper, using the table method:

Pilot . . . . 200 lbs.
Front passenger. . . . . 175 lbs.
Fuel. . . . . 80 gals.
Oil . . . . 12 qts.

CHAPTER SIX
PERFORMANCE

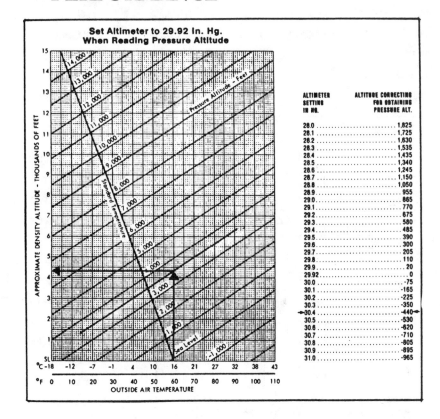

Figure W6-1.

1. Pressure altitude corrected for non-standard temperature is called _____ altitude.

2. As altitude increases, air density (INCREASES / DECREASES).

3. When we refer to high density atitude, we mean that the air is more dense. (TRUE / FALSE)

4. If an airplane stalls at 60 knots indicated airspeed at sea level, its stall speed at 10,000' MSL will be 65 knots. (TRUE / FALSE)

5. Use the chart provided (figure W6-1) and find the density altitude for the following conditions:

FIELD ELEVATION	TEMPER-ATURE	ALTIMETER SETTING	DENSITY ALTITUDE
2,500'	65°F	29.84	_____
6,000'	40°F	29.50	_____
1,500'	85°F	30.20	_____
8,000'	–10°F	30.10	_____

6. You are flying at an indicated altitude of 6,500' with your altimeter set to 30.34. To compute the true airspeed, you need to know the pressure altitude. It is _____.

7. When landing at an airport with an elevation of 4,000' MSL, with an indicated airspeed of 70 knots, the true airspeed is _____ knots. The ground roll after landing will be (LONGER / SHORTER) than at sea level.

8. To clear obstacles after takeoff, you should climb at the best _____ speed.

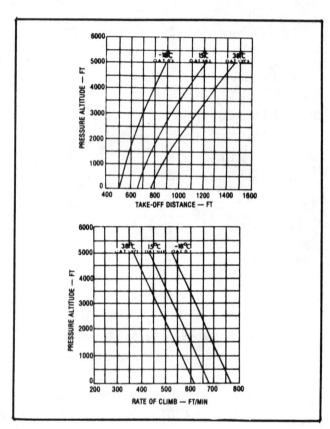

Figure W6-2.

Use the charts (figure W6-2) to answer questions 9 and 10:

9. Determine the takeoff distance and rate of climb. Field elevation is 3,200 feet, altimeter setting is 30.12, and temperature is 59°F.

Distance _____ ft.
Rate of climb _____ FPM

10. Field elevation is 3,860 feet, altimeter setting is 29.78, temperature is 100°F.

Distance _____ ft.
Rate of climb _____ FPM

11. Of the factors listed, which would tend to *decrease* the density altitude at a given airport?

    1. Decreasing barometric pressure.
    2. Increasing relative humidity.
    3. Increasing ambient temperature.
    4. Increasing barometric pressure.

12. Determine the total distance required to land over a 50-foot obstacle from the Landing Distance Chart (figure W6-3):

    Pressure Altitude . . . . 5,000 ft.
    Headwind . . . . 32 KTS
    Temperature . . . . Standard

    1. 239 ft.
    2. 1,099 ft.
    3. 1,291 ft.
    4. 1,434 ft.

13. What is the total landing distance required to clear a 50-foot obstacle with the following conditions using the Landing Distance Chart (figure W6-3)?

    Pressure Altitude . . . . 5,000 ft.
    Headwind. . . . . Calm
    Temperature . . . . 101°F
    Runway . . . . Dry grass

		AT SEA LEVEL & 59° F.		AT 2500 FT. & 50° F.		AT 5000 FT. & 41° F.		AT 7500 FT. & 32° F.	
GROSS WEIGHT LBS.	APPROACH SPEED IAS. MPH	GROUND ROLL	TOTAL TO CLEAR 50 FT. OBS.	GROUND ROLL	TOTAL TO CLEAR 50 FT. OBS	GROUND ROLL	TOTAL TO CLEAR 50 FT. OBS	GROUND ROLL	TOTAL TO CLEAR 50 FT. OBS
1600	60	445	1075	470	1135	495	1195	520	1255

—LANDING DISTANCE— FLAPS LOWERED TO 40° — POWER OFF / HARD SURFACE RUNWAY — ZERO WIND

NOTES: 1. Decrease the distances shown to 10% for each 4 knots of headwind.
2. Increase the distance by 10% for each 60°F temperature increase above standard.
3. For operation on a dry, grass runway, increase distances (both "ground roll" and "total to clear 50 ft. obstacle") by 20% of the "total to clear 50 ft. obstacle" figure.

Figure W6-3.

1. 837 ft.
2. 956 ft.
3. 1,076 ft.
4. 1,554 ft.

14. The phenomenon of _____ may cause an airplane to become airborne before reaching recommended takeoff speed.

15. Refer to the Cruise and Range Performance chart (figure W6-4): You plan to cruise at 5,000 feet, using 75% BHP (brake horsepower) and 2,600

CRUISE & RANGE PERFORMANCE GROSS WEIGHT: 2300 LBS. STANDARD CONDITIONS ZERO WIND LEAN MIXTURE

NOTE: MAXIMUM CRUISE IS NORMALLY LIMITED TO 75% POWER.

ALT	RPM	% BHP	TAS MPH	GAL / HOUR	38 GAL (NO RESERVE)		48 GAL (NO RESERVE)	
					ENDR HOURS	RANGE MILES	ENDR HOURS	RANGE MILES
2500	2700	86	134	9.7	3.9	525	4.9	660
	2600	79	129	8.6	4.4	570	5.6	720
	2500	72	123	7.8	4.9	600	6.2	760
	2400	65	117	7.2	5.3	620	6.7	780
	2300	58	111	6.7	5.7	630	7.2	795
	2200	52	103	6.3	6.1	625	7.7	790
5000	2700	82	134	9.0	4.2	565	5.3	710
	2600	75	128	8.1	4.7	600	5.9	760
	2500	68	122	7.4	5.1	625	6.4	790
	2400	61	116	6.9	5.5	635	6.9	805
	2300	55	108	6.5	5.9	635	7.4	805
	2200	49	100	6.0	6.3	630	7.9	795
7500	2700	78	133	8.4	4.5	600	5.7	755
	2600	71	127	7.7	4.9	625	6.2	790
	2500	64	121	7.1	5.3	645	6.7	810
	2400	58	113	6.7	5.7	645	7.2	820
	2300	52	105	6.2	6.1	640	7.7	810
10,000	2650	70	129	7.6	5.0	640	6.3	810
	2600	67	125	7.3	5.2	650	6.5	820
	2500	61	118	6.9	5.5	655	7.0	830
	2400	55	110	6.4	5.9	650	7.5	825
	2300	49	100	6.0	6.3	635	8.0	800

Figure W6-4.

RPM. How long could the airplane be flown with 48 gallons of usable fuel on board?

_____ hours.

16. What effect does high density altitude have on propeller efficiency?

1. Increased efficiency due to less friction on the propeller blades.
2. Reduced efficiency because the propeller exerts less force than at lower density altitudes.
3. Reduced efficiency due to the increased force of the thinner air on the propeller.
4. Increased efficiency because the propeller exerts more force on the thinner air.

17. The greatest altitude gain per unit of time is obtained by flying at the best _____ of climb speed.

18. To maintain a constant indicated airspeed during climb, the pitch attitude must be gradually lowered as altitude is gained. (TRUE / FALSE)

19. You can expect your groundspeed to be higher when landing at a high altitude airport than when landing at a sea level airport. (TRUE / FALSE)

CHAPTER SEVEN
PILOTAGE:
NAVIGATION BY
GROUND REFERENCE

1. Lines of _____ on an aeronautical chart run north and south.

2. One minute of _____ on an aeronautical chart is equal to one nautical mile.

3. A course measured with reference to a longitude line on an aeronautical chart is a (TRUE / MAGNETIC) course.

4. The amount of variation to be applied when converting a true course to a magnetic course depends on the heading of the airplane. (TRUE / FALSE)

5. Contour lines placed on a Sectional Aeronautical Chart are to show points of the same

   1. longitude.
   2. variation.
   3. latitude.
   4. elevation above sea level.

6. Refer to Figure W7-1. Total distance from Airport "W" to Airport "X" and then to Airport "Y" is approximately

   1. 73 statute miles.
   2. 84 statute miles.
   3. 167 statute miles.
   4. 116 statute miles.

7. Refer to Figure W7-1. Suppose you fly the traffic pattern at 800 feet AGL at Airport "X," the Tri-County Airport. If the altimeter is properly adjusted to the latest altimeter setting, it would indicate the pattern altitude of

   1. 800 feet.
   2. 1,517 feet.
   3. 2,900 feet.
   4. 4,500 feet.

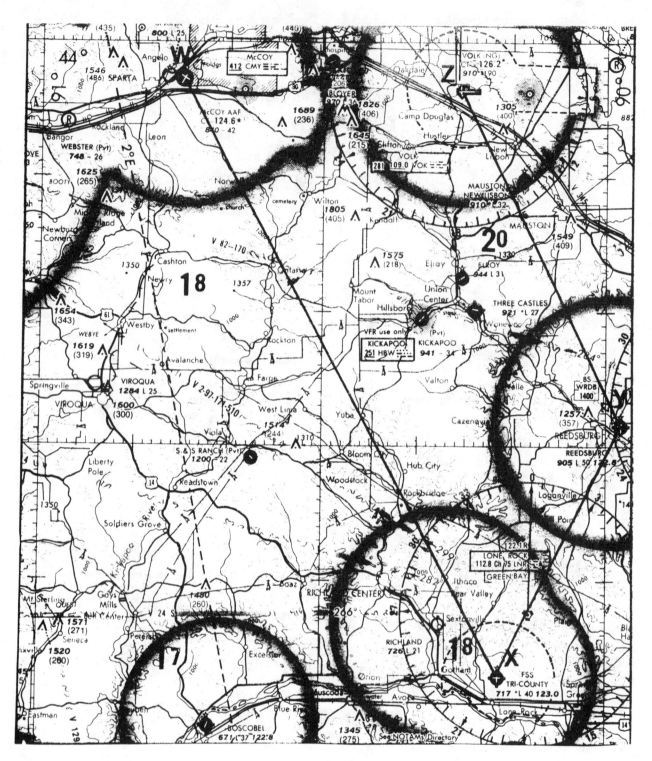

Figure W7-1. Sectional Chart

8. Calculate the magnetic heading and ground-speed for the following conditions:

True course. . . . . 210°
Variation. . . . . 4° East
Cruise altitude . . . . 6,500 feet
Wind. . . . . 240° at 12 KTS
True airspeed. . . . . 160 MPH

1. 220° and 150 MPH.
2. 300° and 160 MPH.
3. 209° and 148 MPH.
4. 200° and 139 MPH.

For questions 9 through 11 refer to Figure W7-1.

9. GIVEN:
True airspeed. . . . . 130 MPH
Forecast winds . . . . from 110° at 15 KTS

What is the magnetic heading and groundspeed from Airport "X" to Airport "W?"

Heading _____
Groundspeed _____

10. What is the estimated time enroute?

_____

11. At a fuel consumption rate of 8.7 gallons per hour, how much fuel is required to be on board in order to land with a 30 minute reserve?

_____

12. How many nautical miles is 160 statute miles equal to? _____

13. GIVEN:
Outside air temperature. +5°C
Pressure altitude . . . . 2,500 ft.
Indicated airspeed. . . . . 150 KTS

Determine the true airspeed.

_____

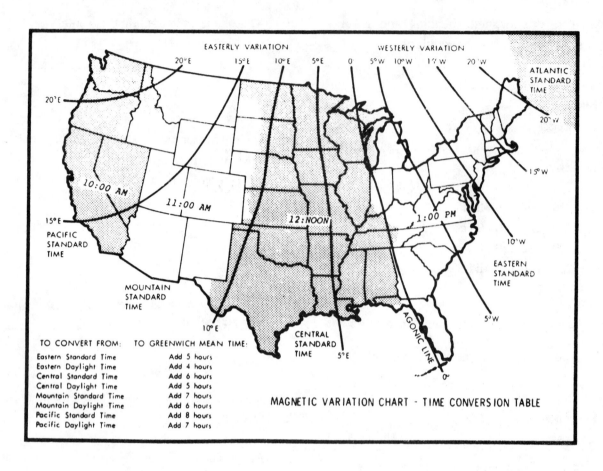

Figure W7-2. Magnetic Variation Chart — Time Conversion Table

14. Refer to the chart (W7-2). Assume that you depart an airport in the Central Daylight Time Zone at 0845 CDT for a 2 hour flight to an airport located in the Mountain Daylight Time Zone. At what Greenwich Mean Time would you expect to land?

_____ Z.

15. Suppose that you depart an airport in the Mountain Standard Time Zone at 1615 MST for a 2 hour 15 minute flight to an airport located in the Pacific Standard Time Zone. What would your estimated time of arrival be at the destination airport?

_____ PST.

CHAPTER EIGHT
RADIO NAVIGATION

1. Select the true statement concerning character-
    istics of VHF radio reception.

    1. VHF reception distance varies in proportion
        to the altitude of the receiving equipment.
    2. Unlike reception with low or medium fre-
        quency equipment, VHF reception is not
        limited to line-of-sight restrictions.
    3. VHF reception distance remains constant
        regardless of altitude.
    4. Reception of VHF signals is more subject to
        signal fades and interference from distant
        stations than reception of low or medium
        frequency signals.

2. When a VOR station is transmitting, but under-
    going adjustment or maintenance, pilots are
    warned of its unreliability by having the
    _____ removed from the
    signal.

3. Fluctuations on the VOR course deviation indi-
    cator needle can be caused by the propeller. (TRUE
    / FALSE)

4. The compass rose printed around a VOR symbol
    on a sectional chart is oriented in relation to (TRUE
    / MAGNETIC) north.

5. Information on unreliable VOR radials can be
    found in the _____
    _____ _____.

VOR RECEIVER CHECK POINTS
VOR/VORTAC

The list of VOR airborne and ground check points are included in this section. Use of these check points is explained in Airman's Information Manual, Basic Flight Information and ATC Procedures.

NOTE: Under column headed "Type Check Pt Gnd AB/ALT", G stands for ground, A, stands for airborne followed by a number (2300) indicating the altitude above mean sea level at which the check should be conducted. Facilities are listed in alphabetical order, in the state where the check points are located

EXCERPTS

Facility Name (arpt name)	Freq/Ident	Type Check Pt. Gnd. AB/ALT	Azimuth from Fac. Mag	Dist. from Fac. N.M.	Check Point Description
NORTH DAKOTA					
Bismarck (Muni Arpt)	116.5/BIS	G	275	4.2	N end ramp area just off apch end rwy 13
Devils Lake	111.0/DVL	A./3000	074	5.0	Over rdo antenna
Dickinson (Muni Arpt)	112.9/DIK	G	182	3.7	Int of E/W twy and N/S twy
Fargo (Hector Fld)	116.2/FAR	A./2000	360	9.4	Over apch end rwy 35
Grand Forks (International Arpt)	109.4/GFK	G	157	1.3	S end of twy parallel to rwy 35
Jamestown (Muni Arpt)	114.5/JMS	G	200	0.6	Twy strip adj to rwy 03
Minot	117.1/MOT	A./2800	091	6.5	Over RR and highway overpass
Williston (Sloulin Fld)	116.3/ISN	A./3000	121	6.2	Over apch end rwy 11
SOUTH DAKOTA					
Aberdeen	113.0/ABR	A./2500	278	7.5	Over grain elev
Brookings	108.8/BKX	A./3000	070	7.5	Over grain elev
Mitchell	109.2/MHE	A./2500	239	10	Over RR and hwy int SW corner of city
Phillip	108.4/PHP	A./3300	156	5.0	Over 2712' twr
Rapid City (Regional Arpt)	112.3/RAP	G	320	4.5	In front of Admin Bldg adj to center twy
Sioux Falls (Joe Foss Fld)	115.0/FSD	G	155	4.7	On W end of Air Ntl Guard parking ramp
	115.0/FSD	G	145	4.4	On E edge of E/W txwy to Gen. Aviation parking ramp
Watertown (Muni Arpt)	116.6/ATY	G	184	3.8	SE corner of term ramp
Winner (Muni Arpt)	112.8/ISD	A./3000	200	8	Over blue water tower S edge of town
Yankton (Chan Gurney Muni Arpt)	111.4/YKN	A./2500	257	6.8	Over twr
WYOMING					
Boysen Reservoir	117.8/BOY	A./6500	180	25	Over Riverton VOR
Casper (Air Trml)	116.2/CPR	A./6400	201	13	Over intersection rwys 21-25-30
Cherokee (Rawlins Muni Arpt)	112.2/CKW	A./7800	065	17	Over FSS bldg
Gillette (Gillette-Campbell County Arpt)	112.5/GCC	G	147	0.7	Runup pad for rwy 33
Laramie (Brees Field)	117.6/LAR	A./8300	112	6.5	Over smoke stack of cement factory
Rock Springs (Sweetwater Co. Arpt)	114.7/RKS	G	266	1.9	In center of turn-around E end rwy 25
	114.7/RKS	G	261	3.1	In center of turn-around W end rwy 07
Sheridan (County Arpt)	115.3/SHR	A./5000	122	5	Over center of apch end rwy 13

Figure W8-1.

Refer to the VOR RECEIVER CHECK POINTS excerpt from the Airport/Facility Directory (figure W8-1) for questions 6 through 8.

6. Which of the following statements is true?

    1. In Rock Springs, WY, there is an airborne checkpoint located over Sweetwater County Airport 1.9 miles from the facility in the center of a turn-around east of Runway 25.
    2. At Yankton, SD, the airborne checkpoint is located 6.8 nautical miles from the facility.
    3. At Joe Foss Field in Sioux Falls, SD, there are both ground and airborne checkpoints.

4. At Mitchell, SD, a ground checkpoint is located 10 nautical miles from the facility on a magnetic bearing of 239°.

7. When an airplane located at the ground checkpoint in Jamestown, ND, has its VOR CDI needle centered with an omni bearing of 200° selected, the TO-FROM indicator will read _____.

8. An airplane flying over the FSS building at Cherokee, WY, on an easterly heading has the CDI needle centered and a TO indication on the omni. The OBS is set to _____.

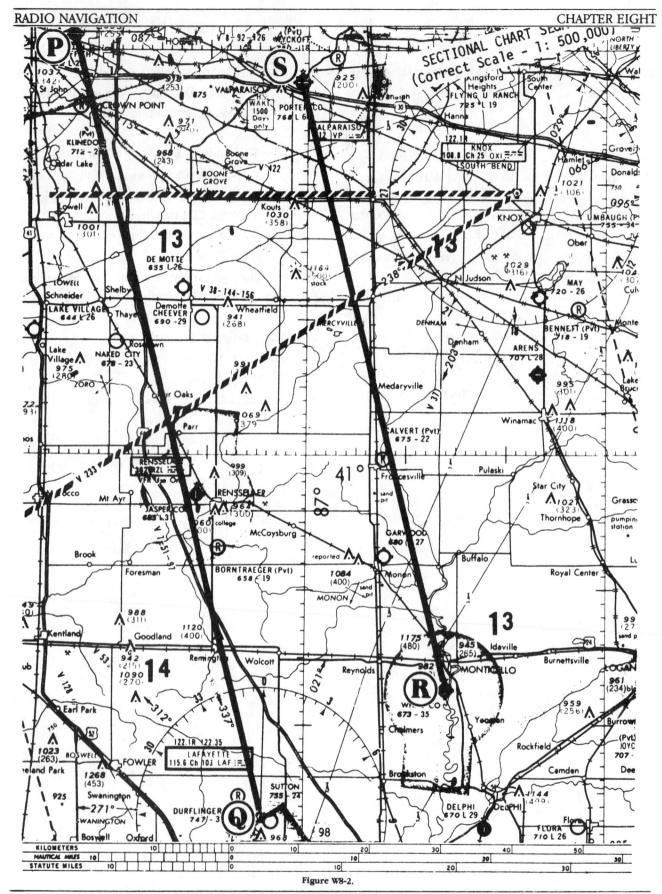

Figure W8-2.

Refer to the chart (figure W8-2) for questions 9 through 12.

9. Departing airport "Q" for airport "P," you should tune your VOR receiver to 115.6 MHz and adjust the omnibearing selector to _____°.

10. If the wind drifts your airplane over the Borntraeger private airport, the CDI needle will be deflected to the _____.

11. You tune your #2 VOR receiver to 108.8 MHz (Knox VORTAC) and select the 238° radial. The CDI needle swings to the right. Have you passed the 238° radial? (YES / NO)

12. You cross the Knox 238° radial at 0810 CST and the Knox 270° radial 13 minutes later. If you maintain the same groundspeed, you should arrive at airport P at _____ CST.

13. Assume that you desire to fly inbound to a VOR station on the 300° radial. The recommended procedure is to set the course selector to

    1. 120° and make heading corrections toward the CDI needle.
    2. 120° and make heading corrections away from the CDI needle.
    3. 300° and make heading corrections toward the CDI needle.
    4. 300° and make heading corrections away from the CDI needle.

14. When using a VOT signal to check the accuracy of your VOR receiver, the needle should center within ±4° of _____° TO or _____° FROM.

15. The angle between the nose of the airplane and the ADF needle is called the _____ bearing to the station.

16. An ADF needle indication directly toward the left wing would be a relative bearing of _____°.

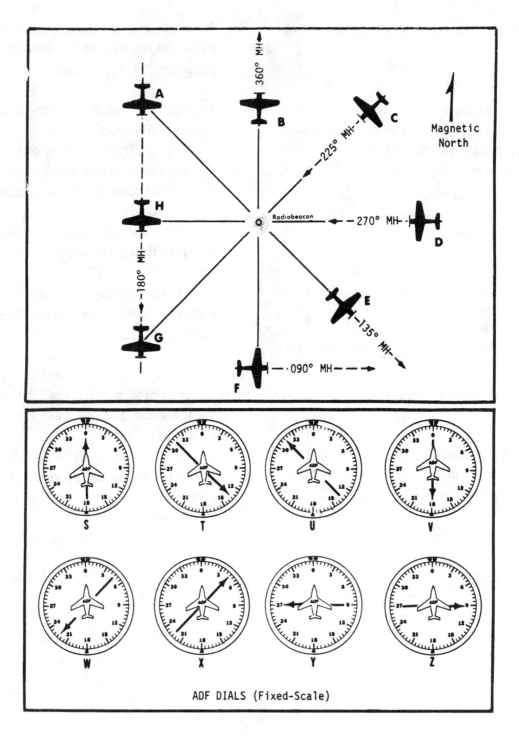

Figure W8-3.

Refer to the illustration (figure W8-3) for questions 17 through 20.

17. Assume that you are flying on a magnetic heading of 180° as depicted by positions A, H, and G. Which indicator matches the ADF indications you would have at each position?

A _____ .
H _____
G _____

18. Which aircraft in the illustration would have ADF indication W?

_____

19. Which ADF indication would the pilot of airplane F have?

_____ .

20. Which airplane(s) would have ADF indication V?

_____ .

21. When using RNAV, the position defined by a radial and distance from a VORTAC is called a

_____ .

22. Area navigation works equally well with either a VOR or a VORTAC. (TRUE / FALSE)

23. The navigation system which electronically "relocates" VORTACs to define a direct route is called

_____ .

24. A position fix can be obtained from the signal of a single VORTAC. (TRUE / FALSE)

25. Loran-C is limited to line-of-sight distances. (TRUE / FALSE)

26. A position fix can be obtained by using signals from the master and one secondary of a Loran-C chain. (TRUE / FALSE)

27. All Loran-C stations transmit on one frequency: _____ KHz.

28. The area of *least* accuracy in Loran-C navigation is along the _____ .

CHAPTER NINE
RADIO COMMUNICATIONS

1. A UNICOM station must provide wind and runway in use information before a pilot can land at an uncontrolled airport. (TRUE / FALSE)

2. Which of the following frequencies is available at most Flight Service Stations?

   1. 122.8 MHz.
   2. 122.9 MHz.
   3. 122.2 MHz.
   4. 121.9 MHz.

3. The frequency to be used when broadcasting "in the blind" at an airport with no radio facility is _____ MHz.

4. 122.75 MHz may be used for air-to-air communication. (TRUE / FALSE)

5. It is possible to communicate with many Flight Service Stations by transmitting on _____ MHz and listening on the appropriate VOR frequency.

6. The International Calling and Distress frequency is _____ MHz.

7. Emergency Locator Transmitters (ELTs) broadcast on _____ MHz (VHF) and _____ MHz (UHF).

8. After landing at a tower-controlled airport, when should you contact ground control?

   1. Prior to turning off the runway.
   2. After reaching a taxi strip that leads directly to the parking area.
   3. After leaving the runway and crossing the runway holding lines.
   4. When the tower instructs you to do so.

```
§   RAPID CITY REGIONAL  (RAP) 7.8 SE  GMT-7(-6DT)  44°02'36"N 103°03'26"W          CHEYENNE
    3182    B   S4  FUEL 100,  JET A  OX 1   CFR Index B                          H-1C, L-9D, 11A
    RWY 14-32: H7422X150 (ASPH)  S-120, D-148, DT-220  HIRL                              9AP
      RWY 14: REIL, VASI.   RWY 32: MALSR.
    RWY 01-19: 2200X200 (TURF)
    AIRPORT REMARKS: Attended 1300-0500Z‡. Rwy lgts opr dusk-0500Z‡. For rwy lgts 0500-1300Z‡ ctc FSS. Porous
      friction course Rwy 14-32 entire length and width. S 2200' Rwy 1-19 open on req only.
    COMMUNICATIONS: UNICOM 123.0
    RAPID CITY FSS (RAP) on arpt 122.65 122.2 122.1R 112.3T (605) 342-2280
  ® ELLSWORTH APP CON 119.5 125.3
    TOWER 118.7 opr 1300-0500Z‡, FSS provides AAS on 118.7 when ATCT clsd.    GND CON 121.9
  ® ELLSWORTH DEP CON 119.5 125.3
    STAGE II SVC ctc APP CON on 119.5
    RADIO AIDS TO NAVIGATION:
      (H) DVORTAC 112.3 RAP Chan 70 43°58'34"N 103°00'43"W 322° 3.8 NM to fld
      NDB (H-SAB) 254 ■ RAP  44°03'16"N 103°05'33"W  103° 1.7 NM to fld.
      ILS 109.3 I-RAP Rwy 32
```

Figure W9-1.

9. The letters "VHF/DF" appearing in the Airport/
    Facility Directory for a certain airport indicate that

    1. this airport is designated as an Airport of
        Entry.
    2. The Flight Service Station has equipment
        with which to determine your direction
        from the station.
    3. this airport has a direct-line phone to the
        Flight Service Station.
    4. this airport is a defense facility.

10. Pilots of aircraft arriving or departing certain high
    activity terminal areas can receive continuous
    broadcasts concerning essential but routine infor-
    mation by using

    1. Aeronautical Advisory Stations (UNICOM).
    2. Automatic Terminal Information Service
        (ATIS).
    3. Aeronautical Multicom Service.
    4. Radar Traffic Information Service.

11. There is no advantage to turning on your trans-
    ponder unless you desire radar traffic advisories.
    (TRUE / FALSE)

12. The altitude reporting capability of your trans-
    ponder can be used if an altitude encoding
    altimeter is installed. This is Mode _____
    operation.

Refer to the Airport/Facility Directory excerpt (figure
W9-1) for questions 13 through 16.

13. The proper sequence of radio frequencies to be
    used at Rapid City Regional Airport to contact
    ground control, the tower, and then the FSS
    would be

    1. 121.9, 119.5, 121.5 MHz.
    2. 121.9, 118.7, 122.2 MHz.
    3. 119.5, 118.7, 1221.R MHz.
    4. 118.7, 121.9, 112.3 MHz.

14. Radar advisories and sequencing are available
    from Ellsworth Departure Control on _____
    MHz.

15. Rapid City UNICOM can provide weather and runway information on 123.0 MHz. (TRUE / FALSE)

16. When the Rapid City Tower is not in operation, contact the FSS on _____ MHz for Airport Advisory Service.

CHAPTER TEN
AIRPORT OPERATIONS
GENERAL

1. When there are no traffic pattern indicators at an uncontrolled airport, a pilot should fly a (RIGHT / LEFT) hand traffic pattern.

2. When a Flight Service Station is located at an uncontrolled airport, an airport advisory area exists within _____ miles of the airport.

3. Operation of the rotating beacon at an airport in a control zone during the hours of daylight may indicate

    1. counterclockwise flow of traffic is required.
    2. the ground visibility is less than 3 miles and/or the ceiling is less than 1,000 ft.
    3. that right-hand traffic is required.
    4. the airport is closed due to hazardous runway conditions.

4. The numbers on a runway indicate its (TRUE / MAGNETIC) direction to the nearest 10°.

5. The most critical wind condition when taxiing a nosewheel-equipped high-wing airplane is a quartering (HEADWIND / TAILWIND).

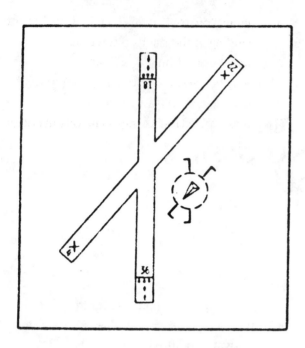

Figure W10-1.

6. If the wind is as shown by the landing direction indicator in figure W10-1, the pilot should land to the

   1. north on Rwy 36 and expect a crosswind from the right.

   2. south on Rwy 18 and expect a crosswind from the right.

   3. southwest on Rwy 22 directly into the wind.

   4. northeast on Rwy 4 directly into the wind.

7. The airplane in position A in figure W10-2 is (ABOVE / BELOW / ON) the glide slope.

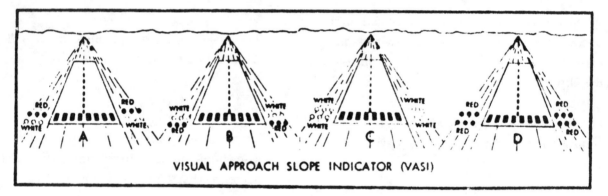

VISUAL APPROACH SLOPE INDICATOR (VASI)

Figure W10-2.

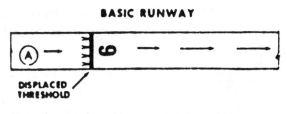

BASIC RUNWAY

DISPLACED
THRESHOLD

Figure W10-3.

8. Refer to the displaced threshold for Runway 9 above (figure W10-3). That portion of the runway identified by the letter "A"

1. is an "overrun area" that is available for landing at the pilot's discretion.

2. may be used only for landings.

3. may be used for taxiing but should not be used for takeoffs or landings.

4. may be used for taxiing or takeoff but not for landing.

CHAPTER ELEVEN
WEATHER

1. The basic source of weather on earth is the heating effect of the sun's rays. (TRUE / FALSE)

2. Descending air creates a (HIGH / LOW) pressure area.

3. Select the true statement concerning wind circulation associated with pressure systems in the Northern Hemisphere.

    1. Wind circulates counterclockwise around high pressure areas and clockwise around low pressure areas.
    2. Wind circulates clockwise around high pressure areas and counterclockwise around low pressure areas.
    3. Wind circulates counterclockwise around both high and low pressure areas.
    4. Wind circulates clockwise around both high and low pressure areas.

4. Refer to the symbols in figure W11-1. The three principal types of fronts are the cold front, the warm front, and the stationary front. Which of the following symbols are properly identified?

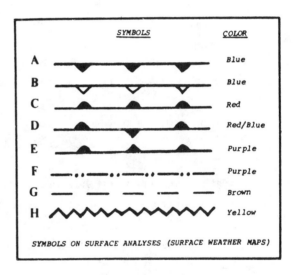

Figure W11-1.

1. A—warm front; B—stationary front; E—cold front.
2. B—cold front; D—warm front; E—stationary front.
3. A—cold front; C—warm front; D—stationary front.
4. C—cold front; D—warm front; E—stationary front.

5. When a cold air mass overtakes and replaces a warm air mass, the resulting weather front is a _____ front.

6. Air which is warmer and less dense than the surrounding air will (RISE / DESCEND). This is a sign of (STABILITY / INSTABILITY).

7. The rotation of the earth causes air movement to be deflected from a direct path from high to low pressure. This is called _____ _____.

8. When a cold front overtakes a warm front an _____ _____ front is formed.

9. Clouds with extensive vertical development are called _____ clouds.

10. Clouds composed largely of ice crystals are _____ clouds.

11. The base of a cloud layer is where the temperature/dewpoint spread is _____°.

12. Warming an air mass (INCREASES / DECREASES) the amount of moisture that it can hold.

13. Regarding the characteristics and weather associated with a warm front, which of the following is a true statement?

    1. The presence of thunderstorms in a warm front is usually easy to detect, since they are not embedded in cloud masses.
    2. The frontal zone may have zero ceiling and zero visibilities over a wide area.

    3. Colder air is overtaking and replacing warmer air and this usually produces wide bands of precipitation ahead of the warm front surface position.
    4. Squall lines sometimes develop 300 miles ahead of warm fronts.

14. When air temperature increases with altitude a temperature inversion is said to exist. 4(TRUE / FALSE)

15. A squall line is usually associated with

    1. a fast-moving cold front.
    2. a fast-moving warm front.
    3. a stationary front.
    4. an occluded front.

16. Precipitation which falls from a cloud and evaporates before it hits the surface is called _____ _____ and should be avoided, as it is a sign of a downdraft.

17. If the temperature at 5,000' is 42° and the dewpoint is 39°, clouds will form if the temperature changes to _____°.

18. Visibility behind a cold front is (GOOD / POOR).

19. If isobars are widely spread on a surface weather map, strong winds may be expected. (TRUE / FALSE)

20. A SIGMET warns of weather hazardous to (ALL / SMALL) aircraft.

21. A continuous weather broadcast on a VOR or NDB frequency is called a _____.

22. A thin, broken layer of clouds (—BKN) constitutes a ceiling (TRUE / FALSE).

23. An advancing warm front that has moist and stable air is characterized, in part, by

    1. a wall of turbulent clouds known as a "squall line."
    2. stratiform clouds and smooth air.
    3. thunderstorms embedded in the cloud masses.
    4. tornadic activity and extensive electrical discharges.

24. In regard to flying in the vicinity of thunderstorms, you should know that

    1. avoidance of lightning and hail is assured by flying in the clear air outside the confines of the thunderstorm cell.
    2. the overhanging anvil of a thunderstorm points in the direction from which the storm has moved.
    3. the most severe conditions, such as heavy hail, destructive winds, and tornadoes are generally associated with squall line thunderstorms.
    4. avoidance of severe turbulence is assured by circumnavigating thunderstorms and clearing edges of the storms by 5 miles.

25. Structural icing can be avoided by staying clear of clouds. (TRUE / FALSE)

26. Warm, moist air over low, flatland areas on clear, calm nights will form _____ fog.

27. What types of fog depend on a wind in order to exist?

    1. Radiation fog and ice fog.
    2. Steam fog and downslope fog.
    3. Precipitation-induced fog and ground fog.
    4. Advection fog and upslope fog.

28. Values used in Winds Aloft Forecasts are (TRUE / MAGNETIC) direction and velocity in (KNOTS / MPH).

29. To determine areas of IFR, and MVFR weather, you would consult a _____ _____-chart.

30. Location of lines and cells of hazardous thunderstorms will be found on a _____ _____ chart.

31. A report of severe icing would be found in a (SIGMET / AIRMET).

CHAPTER TWELVE
PUBLICATIONS

1. A pilot seeking information on arrival or departure procedures should refer to the _____ _____ _____.

2. Information on parachute jumping areas is found in the _____.

3. An Advisory Circular has the force of a regulation. (TRUE / FALSE)

4. FAA Advisory Circulars (some free, others at cost) are available to all pilots and are obtained by

   1. distribution from the nearest FAA District Office.
   2. ordering those desired.
   3. subscribing to the Federal Register.
   4. subscribing to the FAR's.

5. A Pilot/Controller Glossary is contained in the

   1. Airport/Facility Directory.
   2. Federal Aviation Regulations
   3. Airman's Information Manual
   4. Class II Notices to Airmen

§ **JONESBORO** (JBR) 2.6 E GMT-6(-5DT) 35°49'51''N 90°38'47''W   MEMPHIS
    262   B   S4   FUEL 80, 100, JET A +   CFR Index A   H-4F, L-14F
    RWY 05-23: H5599X150 (ASPH) S-80, D-90, DT-140 MIRL   IAP
        RWY 23: VASI
    RWY 14-32: H4101X150 (ASPH) S-30 MIRL
        RWY 14: Thld dsplcd 130'   RWY 32: Railway 700' thld dsplcd 160'
    RWY 18-36: H3943X60 (ASPH) S-30
        RWY 18: Trees 1800'. Thld dsplcd 160'   RWY 36: Bldg 1400' from thld. Thld dsplcd 347'
    AIRPORT REMARKS: Attended 1200-0100Z‡ Control Zone effective 1200-0400Z‡
    COMMUNICATIONS: UNICOM 123.0
        JONESBORO FSS (JBR) on fld 123.6 122.3 122.2 122.1R 108.6T (501) 935-3471
            Opr 1200-0400Z‡. DL dial 0, ask for ENTERPRISE 0246 O/T ctc Memphis FSS
    RADIO AIDS TO NAVIGATION:
        (T) BVOR 108.6 JBR 35°52'30''N 90°35'18''W 222° 3.1 NM to fld Unmonitored 0400-1200Z‡

PINE BLUFF 34°14'48''N 91°55'34''W   MEMPHIS
    (L) BVORTAC 116.0 PBF Chan 107 181° 3.9 NM to Grider Fld   L-14F
        VOR unusable 054°-075° beyond 35 NM below 5000'
                     170°-185° beyond 30 NM below 2000'
                     236°-249° beyond 20 NM below 6000', or beyond 26 NM below 13000'
        TACAN az unusable 091°-129° beyond 20 NM below 3500'

PINE BLUFF
GRIDER FLD (PBF) 4.3 SE GMT-6(-5DT) 34°10'32''N 91°56'07''W   MEMPHIS
    206   B   S4   FUEL 80, 100, JET A   CFR Index A   H-4F, L-14F
    RWY 17-35: H6000X150 (ASPH) S-50, D-70, DT 110 HIRL   IAP
        RWY 17: MALSR, VASI Key 118.4 7 times in 5 sec for high, 5 times in 5 sec for med, 3 times in 5 sec
            for low intensity.
        RWY 35: VASI
    AIRPORT REMARKS: Attended 1300-0500Z‡ On call other hrs. Control Zone effective 1200-0400Z‡
    COMMUNICATIONS:
        LITTLE ROCK FSS (LIT) DL 536-8466
        PINE BLUFF FSS (PBF) 123.6 on arpt (501) 536-8466 Opr 1400-2200Z‡
            Flight planning/briefing svc only
        PINE BLUFF RCO 122.6 122.2 122.1R 116.0T (LITTLE ROCK FSS)
        PINE BLUFF APP/DEP CON 118.4 Opr 1200-0400Z‡
        LITTLE ROCK APP/DEP CON 124.2 0400-1200Z‡
        PINE BLUFF TOWER: 118.4 Opr 1200-0400Z‡ GND CON: 122.7
    RADIO AIDS TO NAVIGATION:
        PINE BLUFF (L) BVORTAC 116.0 PBF Chan 107 34°14'48''N 91°55'34''W 181° 3.9 NM to fld
            VOR unusable 054°-075° beyond 35 NM below 5000'
                         170°-185° beyond 30 NM below 2000'
                         236°-249° beyond 20 NM below 6000', or beyond 26 NM below 13000'
            TACAN az unusable 091°-129° beyond 20 NM below 3500'
        ILS 111.7 I-PBF RWY 17 LOC only

LITTLE ROCK 34°40'39''N 92°10'49''W   MEMPHIS
    (H) BVORTAC 113.9 (LIT) Chan 86 315° 3.8 NM to Adams Fld   H-4F, L-14E

LITTLE ROCK FSS (LIT) on Adams Fld   MEMPHIS
    122.55, 122.35, 122.2, 122.1R, 113.9T (501) 376-0721   H-4B, L-14E

LITTLE ROCK
§ **ADAMS FIELD** (LIT) 1.7 E GMT-6(-5DT) 34°43'48''N 92°13'59''W   MEMPHIS
    257   B   S4   FUEL 80, 100 JET A   OX 1, 3   LRA   CFR Index C   H-4B, L-14E
    RWY 04-22: H7010X150 (ASPH) S-70, D-90, DT-140 HIRL   IAP
        RWY 04: SSALR Thld dsplcd 127'   RWY 22: MALSR VASI
    RWY 17-35: H5125X150 (ASPH) S-30, D-45, DT-70 MIRL
        RWY 17: Road 260'. Thld dsplcd 270'   RWY 35: Road 33' ALSF1
    RWY 14-32: H4032X150 (ASPH) S-26 MIRL
        RWY 14: Road 220' Thld dsplcd 365'   RWY 32: Trees 3000'
    AIRPORT REMARKS: Landing fee. Rwy 14-32 closed to air carriers.
        Transient acft parking at airline terminal ramp ctc arpt police at airline concourse for reentry to locked
        operations area.
    COMMUNICATIONS: ATIS 125.6 1200-0600Z‡ UNICOM 123.0
        LITTLE ROCK FSS (LIT) on fld. 122.55 122.35 122.2 122.1R 113.9T (501) 376-0721
      ® LITTLE ROCK APP CON: 124.2 042°-221° 119.5 222°-041° 118.1
        TOWER: 118.7 123.85 GND CON: 121.9
      ® LITTLE ROCK DEP CON: 124.2 041°-220° 119.5 221°-040° 118.1
        STAGE III SVC ctc APP CON 20 NM, check ATIS
    RADIO AIDS TO NAVIGATION:
        LITTLE ROCK (H) BVORTAC 113.9 LIT Chan 86 34°40'39''N 92°10'49''W 315° 3.8 NM to fld.
        LASKY NDB (H-SAB) 353 LI 34°57'09''N 92°01'09''W 041° 4.6 NM to fld
        ILS 110.3 J-LIT Rwy 04 LOM LASKY NDB
            110.3 I-AAY Rwy 22
        ASR

NOTE: AN AIRPORT/FACILITY DIRECTORY
        LEGEND IS INCLUDED IN THE BACK
        PORTION OF THIS BOOKLET.

Figure W12-1.

Refer to the excerpt from the Airport/Facility Directory (figure W12-1) for questions 6 through 12. The legend is contained in this chapter.

6. Which statement is true regarding the Jonesboro Airport?

   1. Runway 36 threshold is displaced 347 feet.
   2. For Airport Advisory Service contact UNICOM on 122.8 MHz.
   3. Aircraft and powerplant maintenance is not available.
   4. The airport elevation is 2,620 feet MSL.

7. Which statement is true regarding Grider Field at Pine Bluff?

   1. The control tower is in operation 24 hours each day.
   2. There is a rotating beacon at this airport.
   3. The VORTAC facility is located on the airport.
   4. Grade 115 fuel is available.

8. Grider Field has one hard surfaced runway. (TRUE / FALSE)

9. The longest runway at Jonesboro Airport has a VASI on each end. (TRUE / FALSE)

10. Concerning Adams Field at Little Rock, which statement is true?

    1. The airport elevation is 1,700 feet MSL.
    2. The airport has a rotating beacon in operation from dusk to dawn.
    3. Runway 35 has a VASI installation.
    4. The full length of Runway 17 is available for takeoffs and landings.

11. Regarding the three airports listed, only _____ has ATIS.

12. There are no obstructions in the approach path to Runway 35 at Adams Field. (TRUE / FALSE)

CHAPTER THIRTEEN
PHYSICAL EFFECTS

1. You may experience "the bends" if you fly within
_____ hours of scuba diving.

2. Assume that during a night flight you lose all outside visual references and become spatially disoriented. In this situation you are probably experiencing

   1. mild motion sickness.
   2. vertigo.
   3. carbon monoxide poisoning.
   4. the first indication of chronic fatigue.

3. Pilots may not act as flight crewmembers within _____ hours of ingesting an alcoholic beverage.

4. Smokers will experience the symptoms of hypoxia at a (HIGHER / LOWER) altitude than non-smokers.

5. A pilot should be able to overcome the symptoms or avoid future occurrences of hyperventilation by

   1. closely monitoring the flight instruments to control the airplane.
   2. slowing the breathing rate, breathing into a bag, or talking aloud.
   3. increasing the breathing rate in order to increase lung ventilation.
   4. refraining from the use of over-the-counter remedies and drugs such as antihistamines, cold tablets, tranquilizers, etc.

6. The effect on judgment and decision-making ability of alcohol or drugs is intensified by altitude. (TRUE / FALSE)

7. The best way to overcome the effects of vertigo is to

   1. depend on sensations received from fluid in the semicircular canals of the middle ear.
   2. concentrate on any "yaw," "pitch" and "roll" sensations.
   3. consciously slow your breathing rate until symptoms clear and then resume normal breathing rate.
   4. rely upon the aircraft instrument indications.

8. The substance in the blood which absorbs oxygen is called _____.

9. The symptoms of carbon monoxide poisoning will diminish as soon as you are able to land and breathe fresh air. (TRUE / FALSE)

10. Drinking black coffee will counteract the effects of drinking before flying. (TRUE / FALSE)

11. Which statement is true regarding hypoxia?

    1. Avoid flying above 10,000 feet MSL for prolonged periods without breathing supplemental oxygen.

    2. rely on your body's built-in alarm system to warn when you are not getting enough oxygen.

    3. try swallowing, yawning, or holding the mouth and nose shut and forcibly try to exhale.

    4. avoid hyperventilation which is caused by rapid heavy breathing, and results in excess carbon dioxide in the bloodstream.

12. A pilot can only be grounded for medical reasons by an Aviation Medical Examiner. (TRUE / FALSE)

CHAPTER FOURTEEN
NATIONAL AIRSPACE
SYSTEM

1. A pilot must be instrument rated and have an instrument clearance to enter Terminal Control Area. (TRUE / FALSE)

2. You are flying in clear skies over an airport that has a control zone. The ceiling at that airport is reported to be 800' broken clouds. You do not need to communicate with any agency for clearance through the control zone. (TRUE / FALSE)

3. During operations *within controlled airspace* at altitudes of more than 1,200' AGL but less than 10,000' MSL, the minimum "distance above clouds" requirement for VFR flight is

   1. 500 feet.
   2. 1,000 feet.
   3. 1,500 feet.
   4. 2,000 feet.

4. Only pilots who hold instrument ratings may receive Special VFR clearance at night. (TRUE / FALSE).

5. When operating an airplane within a control zone under Special VFR, the flight visibility should be at least

   1. 1 statute mile.
   2. 3 statute miles.
   3. 5 statute miles.
   4. 7 statute miles.

6. Circle those airspace designations which require permission or a clearance for entry under VFR conditions.

   Military Operating Area
   Terminal Control Area
   Warning Area
   Positive Control Area
   Restricted Area
   Control Zone
   Control Area
   Continental Control Area

7. Which of the following statements is true regarding the requirements for operating within a Group I Terminal Control Area?

A. The pilot must hold at least a Commercial Pilot Certificate.

B. Authorization from ATC is required prior to operating in the area.

C. The pilot must be instrument rated and must be operating on an instrument flight plan.

D. The airplane must have an operable VOR receiver, two-way communications radio, and a radar beacon transponder.

E. The pilot in command must hold at least a Private Pilot Certificate to take off or land within the TCA.

The true statements are

1. A, C, D.
2. C, D, E.
3. B, D, E.
4. A, B, C, D.

8. Aircraft speed is unlimited above _____ feet MSL.

9. Required flight visibility is 1 mile both below and above 1,200' AGL in _____ airspace.

10. When flying more than 10,000' MSL you must stay _____ below, _____ above, and _____ horizontally from all clouds.

11. To operate an airplane VFR *outside controlled airspace* at more than 1,200 above the surface but less than 10,000' MSL, the minimum distance below or above the clouds is

1. 500 feet below or 500 feet above.
2. 500 feet below or 1,000 feet above.
3. not specified by regulations.
4. 1,000 feet below or 500 feet above the clouds.

12. Permission to transit a Prohibited Area can be obtained from the controlling agency or through the FSS. (TRUE / FALSE)

13 **To enter or depart an airport within a Control Zone when the weather is reported to be 900 overcast with 2 miles visibility, you need a clearance from Air Traffic Control. (TRUE / FALSE).**

14. A Control Area with a floor of controlled airspace at 700' AGL is colored _____ on all sectional charts.

15. In mountainous areas the floor of controlled airspace is designated on sectional charts. (TRUE / FALSE)

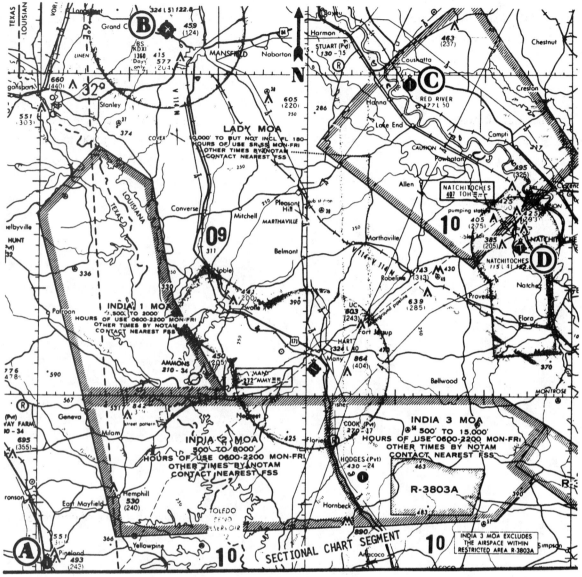

Figure W14-1.

16. Refer to the chart excerpt (figure W14-1). Concerning the LADY MOA and a proposed flight from airport "B" to airport "D," select the true statement.

1. You should circumnavigate the MOA by flying around the southern tip of it.

2. Between Mondays and Fridays a pilot should contact the nearest FSS for rerouting around the area for a flight to airport "D."

3. Nonparticipating IFR traffic may be cleared through the MOA, and VFR pilots should exercise caution while flying within the area.

4. The appropriate military authority having jurisdiction over the area must be contacted to obtain permission to fly within the area.

CHAPTER FIFTEEN
REGULATIONS

PART 61

1. When acting as a required flight crewmember you must have in your possession your pilot and medical certificates. (TRUE / FALSE)

2. To act as pilot in command of an aircraft carrying passengers at night, you must have performed, within the preceding 90 days, three takeoffs and landings

   1. to a full stop, at night, in the same category and class of aircraft to be used.
   2. to a full stop, day or night, in any aircraft.
   3. touch and go or full stop, at night, in any aircraft.
   4. touch and go or full stop, either day or night, in any aircraft.

3. Pilot certificates (other than student pilot certificates) have no expiration date. (TRUE / FALSE).

4. Which of the following is an aircraft category rating?

   1. multiengine land.
   2. free balloon.
   3. rotorcraft.
   4. seaplane.

5. You hold a private pilot certificate with a single engine land rating. Can you fly a single engine seaplane solo? (YES / NO).

6. In order to act as pilot in command of a turbojet or large (more than 12,500 lb) airplane, you must hold a _____ for that airplane.

7. A Third Class medical certificate issued on May 12, 1985, will become invalid on _____ _____, _____.

8. A pilot holding a First Class medical certificate issued eleven months preceding the date of flight can act as a commercial pilot on that flight. (TRUE / FALSE)

9. Assume that you were issued a Third Class medical certificate 15 months ago. To act as pilot in command, this medical certificate

    1. has expired, therefore you cannot act as pilot in command, but you can serve as a crewmember.
    2. is current, and can be used to exercise all of the privileges of a private pilot.
    3. has expired, and you cannot exercise the privileges of a private pilot.
    4. is current, but limits your flights to solo only.

10. If your biennial flight review has expired you are limited to fly solo only. (TRUE / FALSE)

11. Any deviation from the Federal Aviation Regulations, even in an emergency, requires a report to the FAA. (TRUE / FALSE)

12. You do not meet the recency of experience requirement for night flight carrying passengers and official sunset is 1900. You must be on the ground by _____ to comply with regulations.

13. According to regulations pertaining to general privileges and limitations, a private pilot may

    1. charge a reasonable fee for acting as pilot in command.
    2. share the operating expenses of a flight with the passengers.
    3. be paid for the operating expenses of a flight if at least three takeoffs and landings were made by the pilot within the preceding 90 days.
    4. not be paid in any manner for the expenses of a flight.

14. A pilot proficiency check such as a flight test for a new certificate or rating can substitute for a biennial flight review. (TRUE / FALSE)

15. A biennial flight review expires

    1. at the end of the 24th month following a biennial flight review or pilot proficiency check.
    2. 24 months from the date of a biennial flight review or pilot proficiency check.

16. A private pilot who meets the recency of experience requirements and has a current biennial flight review can act as pilot in command of a high performance airplane without further qualification. (TRUE / FALSE)

PART 91

17. While the pilot must wear a seatbelt during takeoffs and landings, use of seatbelts is discretionary for passengers. (TRUE / FALSE)

18. During flight, which of these documents is required to be aboard?

    1. Owner's Manual.
    2. Weight and Balance Handbook.
    3. Aircraft and engine logbooks.
    4. Registration Certificate.

19. When directed to take an action by an Air Traffic Controller, a pilot must comply, even though the action appears unsafe or imprudent. (TRUE / FALSE)

20. When planning a cross-country flight a pilot must check both weather reports *and forecasts*. (TRUE / FALSE)

21. In addition to other preflight action for a VFR cross-country flight, regulations specifically require the pilot in command to

    1. file a flight plan for the proposed flight.
    2. check each fuel tank visually to ensure that it is always filled to capacity.
    3. determine runway lengths at airports of intended use.
    4. check the accuracy of the omni receiver-indicator if the flight is to be made on airways.

22. Acrobatic maneuvers are defined as those where the bank angle exceeds _____ ° and/or the nose pitch attitude exceeds _____° up or down.

23. A fuel reserve of 45 minutes is required for (DAY / NIGHT / DAY OR NIGHT) VFR flights.

24. A radar beacon transponder (IS / IS NOT) required for all VFR flights.

25. Flight into a Group II Terminal Control Area requires an altitude reporting transponder. (TRUE / FALSE)

26. An altitude reporting transponder is required for flights above _____' MSL in controlled airspace.

27. Who is responsible for determining whether a rental aircraft is in condition for safe flight?

    1. The pilot in command.
    2. The owner of the aircraft.
    3. The maintenance inspector.
    4. The mechanic who maintains the aircraft.

28. A pilot must use supplemental oxygen at all times when flying above _____ feet MSL.

29. Passengers must use supplemental oxygen when flying at altitudes above 15,000' MSL. (TRUE / FALSE)

30. A multiengine airplane will cross the path of a single engine airplane from left to right at the same altitude. The _____ airplane has the right of way.

31. Aircraft operating in the air must display lighted position lights from 1 hour before sunset to one hour before sunrise. (TRUE / FALSE)

32. VFR flight plans are automatically closed by the tower or FSS at the completion of a flight. (TRUE / FALSE)

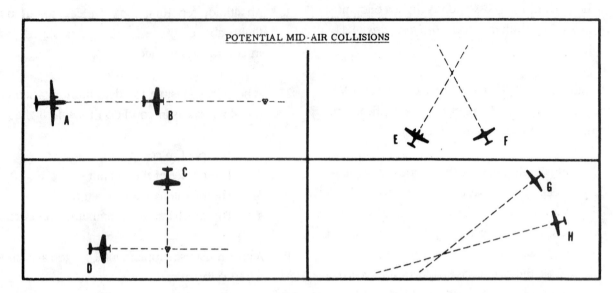

Figure W15-1.

Refer to figure W15-1 for questions 33 through 36.

33. Select the true statement concerning the proper action of airplanes depicted in figure W15-1.

   1. Airplane "H" should alter course since airplane "G" is to its right.
   2. Airplane "F" should alter course since airplane "E" is to its left.
   3. Airplane "D" should alter course since the pilot occupying the left seat has better vision than the pilot of airplane "C."
   4. Airplane "B" should alter course to the left so the faster multiengine airplane "A" might pass.

34. If airplanes "E" and "F" (figure W15-1) were at the same altitude on converging courses, what action should be taken?

   1. Airplane "E" should give way to airplane "F."

2. Airplane "F" should given way to airplane "E."
3. Airplane "F" should give way because multi-engine airplanes have the right-of-way over single-engine airplanes.
4. Airplane "E" should give way because single-engine airplanes have the right-of-way over multiengine airplanes.

35. Airplane "A" (figure W15-1) is overtaking airplane "B," and both are at the same altitude. What action should be taken?

   1. Airplane "A" should descend on course and pass well below airplane "B."
   2. Airplane "A" should alter course to the right and pass well clear of airplane "B."
   3. Airplane "A" should alter course to the left and pass well clear of airplane "B."
   4. Airplane "A" should climb on course and pass well above airplane "B."

36. Airplanes "C" and "D" in figure W15-1 are converging at the same altitude. Which statement is true?

   1. Airplane "C" should gain 500 feet and airplane "D" should lose 500 feet of altitude.
   2. The airplane that is flying on an airway has the right-of-way.
   3. Airplane "D" should alter course since airplane "C" is to its left.
   4. Airplane "C" should alter course since airplane "D" is to its right.

37. When flying over a populated area a pilot must maintain an altitude at least _____ feet above the highest obstacle within _____ horizontally.

38. At no time (except when taking off or landing) may a pilot fly within 500 feet of the surface. (TRUE / FALSE)

39. An alternating red and green light displayed from a tower to an airplane in flight means "_____ _____."

40. The light signal to stop taxiing is a _____ light.

41. A steady white light displayed to an airplane in flight means "return for landing.". (TRUE / FALSE)

42. At an uncontrolled airport, where no traffic pattern indicator is displayed, all turns must be to the _____.

43. An airplane flying more than 3,000 feet AGL on a magnetic (HEADING / COURSE) of 300° must choose a cruising altitude of an (EVEN / ODD) thousand plus 500 feet.

APPENDIX A
ANSWERS AND EXPLANATIONS

1.

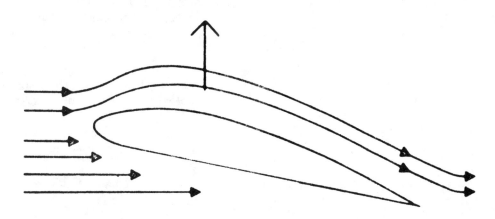

2. Angle of attack; vertical lift; drag; chord line.

3. The 10° angle of attack ... a 20° angle of attack exceeds the stalling angle of attack.

4. The angle of incidence.

5.

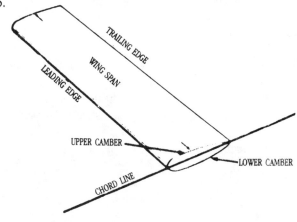

6.

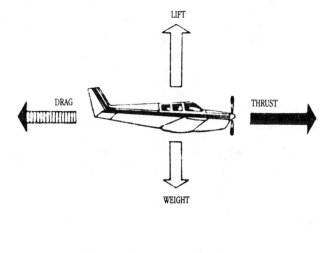

7.

CONTROL SURFACES

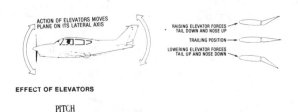

EFFECT OF ELEVATORS

PITCH

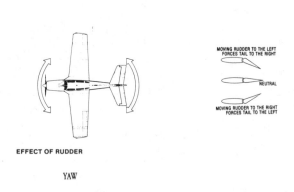

EFFECT OF RUDDER

YAW

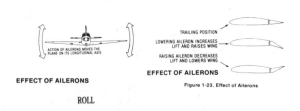

EFFECT OF AILERONS

ROLL

Figure 1-23. Effect of Ailerons

8. Answer #4 is correct. Rate of turn is inversely proportional to airspeed and radius of turn is directly proportional to airspeed.

9. Drag; lift.

10. Stall. A spin results when one wing stalls before the other.

11. False. Moist air is less dense than dry air.

12. Forward.

13. Adverse drag.

14. Parasite; induced.

15. Answer #3 is correct. Torque creates a left-turning tendency when airspeed is low and power setting is high.

16. Answer #3 is correct. Flaps also lower the stalling speed; each increment of flap extension increases the margin between approach speed and stalling speed.

17. Answer #2 is correct. The load factor in a 60° banked turn is two times the force of gravity.

18. Increases. Increasing the angle of attack increases lift, and induced drag is the price you pay for lift.

19. Increase; decrease. A slow airplane can always turn inside of a fast airplane.

20. Opposite to the direction of. A trim tab deflected downward will force its associated control surface upward.

21. Increase. The increased angle of attack required to create the lift to support the increased weight narrows the margin between the cruising angle of attack and the critical stalling angle of attack.

22. Lateral.

23. Answer #4 is correct. The first three answers represent the situations you will experience in training, but there is NO attitude or airspeed at which an inept pilot cannot stall an airplane.

24. Critical.

CHAPTER THREE
ANSWERS AND EXPLANATIONS

1. Lower. NEVER use a fuel grade lower than that specified by the manufacturer.

2. Answer #4 is correct. When the intake air expands in the venturi its temperature decreases.

3. Answer #4 is correct. You are asking the engine to put out too much power with too little fuel for cooling.

4. Rich. Operating with "too much" fuel is inefficient, uneconomical, and leads to spark plug fouling.

5. Answer #2 is correct. If oil temperature is normal you probably just need to add oil.

6. False. The question defines preignition.

7. Detonation.

8. False. This is a major advantage of alternators over generators.

CHAPTER FOUR
ANSWERS AND EXPLANATIONS

1. Answer #2 is correct. The other instruments require static pressure only.

2. Calibrated. The difference between indicated and calibrated airspeed is greatest at slow speeds and is negligible at cruise speeds.

3. 2%. This is a rule of thumb.

4. Answer #3 is correct. When flying at airspeeds in the yellow arc you must exercise caution against sudden control movements and avoid encounters with turbulence.

5. Bottom; white. The white arc is the flap range, and the low speed end is the stalling speed with flaps extended (V_{SO}).

6. Answer #4 is correct. This is the high speed end of the yellow arc.

7. 12,400'.

8. A, B, D, E.

9. Answer #3 is correct. "From high to low, look out below" applies to temperature as well as pressure.

10. Pressure.

11. Density.

12. Answer #2 is correct. When you belatedly set the altimeter from 30.20" to 29.94", the altimeter needles will turn counterclockwise 260' and will then read field elevation at the destination airport.

13. Deviation.

14. True.

15. West. When turning from northerly headings, the compass will at first turn in the opposite direction, stop, and then lag the actual heading of the airplane.

16. South. On both easterly and westerly headings, "accelerate north, decelerate south."

17. W, Y, Z.

18. X.

19. Y.

20. Right. In a slip, the ball falls to the inside of the turn.

CHAPTER FIVE
ANSWERS AND EXPLANATIONS

1. Answer #3 is correct. Empty weight never includes usable fuel.

2. Forward. The CG follows the weight.

3. Arm.

4. Answer #2 is correct. Add the empty weight (1,446), oil (15), and full fuel (352.8) for a total of 1,813.8 lbs. Subtract 1,813.8 from the authorized gross weight of 2,450.

5. Answer #2 is correct. Add the empty weight (1,446), oil (15), baggage (90), and passengers (735) for a total of 2,286. Subtract 2,286 from the authorized gross weight of 2,450. Usable fuel can weigh 164 lbs. or 27.3 gallons at 6 lbs. per gallon.

6. Answer #1 is correct.

7. Answer #1 is correct.

8. Answer #3 is correct.

9. Answer #4 is correct.

10. Answer #3 is correct.

11. No. Total weight is 3,398 and total moment is 2,938.5. CG is out of the envelope aft at 86.48 inches.

12. Yes. Total weight is 2,988 and total moment is 2,337. CG is 78.2".

CHAPTER SIX
ANSWERS AND EXPLANATIONS

1. Density.

2. Decreases.

3. False.

4. True. Indicated stall speed is the same at all altitudes.

5. 3,500'; 7,000'; 3,300'; 5,000'.

6. 6,080. Turning the altimeter setting window from 30.34 to 29.92 will cause the altimeter needles to move counterclockwise 420'.

7. 76 knots, approximately, with a longer ground roll. The "2% per 1,000'" thumb rule is based on an atmosphere that changes density linearly, while the true atmosphere is constantly changing.

8. Angle of climb.

9. 920'; 525 feet/min.

10. 1,300'; 420 ft./min.

11. Answer #4 is correct. Answers #1 through #3 would decrease the density of the air and therefore increase density altitude.

12. Answer #1 is correct. Refer to Note 1 and reduce the zero-wind figure by 80%.

13. Answer #4 is correct. Applying Note 2 gives a distance of 1,314 feet, and applying Note 3 adds an additional 239 feet.

14. Ground effect.

15. 5.9 hours.

16. Answer #2 is correct.

17. Rate of climb.

18. True. Indicated airspeed decreases at the rate of 2% per 1,000', so to maintain a constant indicated airspeed the nose must be lowered.

19. True.

CHAPTER SEVEN
ANSWERS AND EXPLANATIONS

1. Longitude.

2. Latitude.

3. True.

4. False. Heading affects deviation, not variation.

5. Answer #4 is correct.

6. Answer #2 is correct.

7. Answer #2 is correct.

8. Answer #3 is correct. Did you convert the wind to MPH?

9. 334°, 142 MPH (125 knots). True course is measured as 332°, wind correction angle by flight

computer is 5° right or a true heading of 337°. Applying 3° easterly variation gives a magnetic heading of 334°.

10. A distance of 59 statute miles will be flown in 25 minutes at 142 MPH.

11. 25 minutes at a consumption rate of 8.7 GPH is 3.6 gallons; a 30 minute reserve is 4.35 gallons, for a total of 8 gallons.

12. 139.

13. 154 knots.

14. 1545Z.

15. 1730 PST.

CHAPTER EIGHT
ANSWERS AND EXPLANATIONS

1. Answer #1 is correct.

2. Identifier.

3. True. Changing the propeller RPM slightly will eliminate the problem.

4. Magnetic.

5. Airport/Facility Directory.

6. Answer #2 is correct.

7. FROM.

8. 245°.

9. 345°.

10. Left.

11. No. If the needle is on the same side as the station, you're not there yet (this only works with FROM indications).

12. 0832CST. Flying 20 miles in 13 minutes takes a groundspeed of 94 knots, and it will take 9

minutes from the 270° radial to Airport P. 0810 + 13 + 9 = 0832.

13. Answer #1 is correct. Flying *inbound* on a radial requires that you fly its reciprocal as a heading.

14. 180°; 360°.

15. Relative.

16. 270.

17. U; Y; W.

18. G.

19. Y.

20. B; E.

21. Waypoint.

22. False.

23. Area navigation

24. True.

25. False.

26. False.

27. 100.

28. Baseline extension.

CHAPTER NINE
ANSWERS AND EXPLANATIONS

1. False.

2. Answer #3 is correct.

3. 122.9 MHz.

4. True.

5. 122.1 MHz.

6. 121.5 MHz (or 243 MHz for UHF, military-only).

7. 121.5; 243.

8. Answer #4 is correct.

9. Answer #2 is correct.

10. Answer #2 is correct.

11. False. You can be pointed out as traffic to other pilots if your transponder is on.

12. C.

13. Answer #2 is correct.

14. 119.5 MHz.

15. False. Only the tower controller can provide this information to pilots; when the tower is closed, the FSS provides this information on the tower frequency.

16. 118.7 MHz.

CHAPTER TEN
ANSWERS AND EXPLANATIONS

1. Left.

2. 10.

3. Answer #2 is correct.

4. Magnetic.

5. Tailwind.

6. Answer #2 is correct. Runway 4-22 is closed.

7. On.

8. Answer #4 is correct.

CHAPTER ELEVEN
ANSWERS AND EXPLANATIONS

1. True.

2. High.

3. Answer #2 is correct.

4. Answer #3 is correct.

5. Cold.

6. Rise; instability.

7. Coriolis Effect.

8. Occluded.

9. Cumulus.

10. Cirrus.

11. 0°.

12. Increases.

13. Answer #2 is correct.

14. True.

15. Answer #1 is correct.

16. Virga.

17. 39°

18. Good.

19. False.

20. All.

21. TWEB (Transcribed Weather Broadcast).

22. False.

23. Answer #2 is correct.

24. Answer #3 is correct.

25. False. Freezing rain can fall into clear air and form on your airplane.

26. Radiation or ground.

27. Answer #4 is correct. Advection is defined as horizontal movement.

28. True; knots.

29. Weather Depiction.

30. Radar Summary.

31. AIRMET.

CHAPTER TWELVE
ANSWERS AND EXPLANATIONS

1. Airman's Information Manual.

2. Airport/Facility Directory.

3. False

4. Answer #2 is correct.

5. Answer #3 is correct.

6. Answer #1 is correct.

7. Answer #2 is correct.

8. True.

9. False.

10. Answer #2 is correct.

11. Adams Field.

12. False.

CHAPTER THIRTEEN
ANSWERS AND EXPLANATIONS

1. 24.

2. Answer #2 is correct.

3. 8 — and this is a minimum!

4. Lower.

5. Answer #2 is correct.

6. True.

7. Answer #4 is correct.

8. Hemoglobin.

9. False.

10. False.

11. Answer #1 is correct.

12. False. By regulation, you must ground yourself if you are taking medication or cannot meet the standards of the medical certificate you hold.

CHAPTER FOURTEEN
ANSWERS AND EXPLANATIONS

1. False.

2. True. A clearance is only required for flight beneath the ceiling.

3. Answer #2 is correct.

4. True.

5. Answer #1 is correct.

6. Terminal Control Area, Positive Control Area, Restricted Area.

7. Answer #3 is correct.

8. 10,000.

9. Uncontrolled.

10. 1,000; 1,000; 1 mile.

11. Answer #3 is correct. The requirement is "clear of clouds."

12. False. You cannot get clearance through a Prohibited Area.

13. True.

14. Magenta.

15. True.

16. Answer #3 is correct.

CHAPTER FIFTEEN
ANSWERS AND EXPLANATIONS

1. True.

2. Answer #1 is correct.

3. True.

4. Answer #3 is correct.

5. Yes. A class rating is required in order to carry passengers.

6. Type rating.

7. At midnight May 31, 1987.

8. True.

9. Answer #2 is correct.

10. False. You are grounded until you receive a satisfactory BFR.

11. False. Only upon the request of the Administrator.

12. 2,000.

13. Answer #2 is correct.

14. True.

15. Answer #1 is correct.

16. False.

17. False.

18. Answer #4 is correct.

19. False.

20. True.

21. Answer #3 is correct.

22. 60; 30.

23. Night.

24. Is not.

25. False.

26. 12,500.

27. Answer #1 is correct.

28. 14,000.

29. False. Passengers must be provided with oxygen but they do not have to use it.

30. Single engine.

31. False. From sunset to sunrise.

32. False.

33. Answer #1 is correct.

34. Answer #1 is correct.

35. Answer #2 is correct.

36. Answer #4 is correct.

37. 1,000; 2,000.

38. False.

39. Exercise extreme caution.

40. Steady red.

41. False.

42. Left.

43. Course; even.

APPENDIX B
TEST TAKING TIPS

If you have digested all of the material we have provided, taking the test will be an anticlimax. You will take the test at an FAA office or at a facility provided by an FAA designated examiner; your instructor should help you make the arrangements. Designated examiners charge a small fee. Be sure that you take evidence of completing a ground school or an instructor's recommendation with you to give to the examiner. If you want to rely solely on this home study course, you must take it to the FAA; they will review it and give you a Written Test Authorization form. Call before taking a home study course to the FAA to ensure that an operations inspector will be available to check the material and issue the form.

You will need a flight computer and plotter; most four-function calculators and electronic flight computers are acceptable, although any computer with a programmable memory will be checked thoroughly by the examiner to be sure you haven't programmed in some answers. Leave all instruction books at home. The examiner will provide scratch paper and pencils.

There will be 60 questions on the examination, selected from the 1,917 in the test booklet. If you are stumped by a question which has been assigned to you, check some of the other questions on the same page. Questions on the same subject are printed together, and you may find a situation like this:

Your question: "To determine pressure altitude, set your altimeter to . . ."

Nearby question: "When an altimeter is set to 29.92, it measures . . ."

All of the chart legend and Airport/Facility Directory legend information you will need is printed in the back of the book, and the answers to many questions will be found in that material.

Do not go through the test booklet one question at a time ... getting hung up on one question can take valuable time. Go through the entire test once, answering all of the questions that you are certain of and marking your answer choice on the question sheet (not the answer sheet). Then go back through the book and work on the tougher ones. Each question is worth 1.6 points, so you should not let one hard question delay you from answering four easy ones. You are allowed four hours for the test.

When you have marked all of your chosen answers on the question sheet, transfer them carefully to the no-carbon answer sheet. Do not make any marks on the answer sheet other than filling in the circles for your answer choices. By following this procedure you will not have any problems with changing answers on the no-carbon answer sheet.